Search for Mother
Journaling

Search for Mother Journaling

Valerie Albrecht

BALBOA.
PRESS

A DIVISION OF HAY HOUSE

Balboa Press books may be ordered through booksellers or by contacting:

Balboa Press
A Division of Hay House
1663 Liberty Drive
Bloomington, IN 47403
www.balboapress.com.au
1 (877) 407-4847

Because of the dynamic nature of the Internet, any web addresses or
links contained in this book may have changed since publication and
may no longer be valid. The views expressed in this work are solely those
of the author and do not necessarily reflect the views of the publisher,
and the publisher hereby disclaims any responsibility for them.

The author of this book does not dispense medical advice or prescribe the use
of any technique as a form of treatment for physical, emotional, or medical
problems without the advice of a physician, either directly or indirectly. The
intent of the author is only to offer information of a general nature to help
you in your quest for emotional and spiritual well-being. In the event you use
any of the information in this book for yourself, which is your constitutional
right, the author and the publisher assume no responsibility for your actions.

Any people depicted in stock imagery provided by Thinkstock are models,
and such images are being used for illustrative purposes only.
Certain stock imagery © Thinkstock.

Printed in the United States of America.

ISBN: 978-1-4525-0166-6 (sc)
ISBN: 978-1-4525-0167-3 (e)

Balboa Press rev. date: 01/16/2015

Contents

The Way Forward Emerges

Search for Mother Journaling

When I look back on my time as a new mother I remember an overabundance of feelings and thoughts, the beauty and innocence on my babies' faces and being exhausted from breast feeding nights. I recall falling in unconditional love with my babies along with falling into despair over mothering expectations, mine and others'. Some days, I did not understand my ways of mothering, or my reactions to my children and my mother. Other days, I understood with both grateful and alarming revelation. Time and again my positive, joyful experiences of mothering and being mothered were overwhelmed by conflicting, confusing emotions and a longing to make sense of "mother".

My first book *Search for Mother* addressed this longing by relating my natural therapy birthing work in Australia, India and North America. It also unearthed profound questions about mother, her forms, her essences and her dualities. Additionally it was an impetus for both men and women readers to share with me fulfilling and heartbreaking searches, connections and disconnections. *Search for Mother* also had the wonderful, unexpected outcome of birthing practitioners and organizations incorporating its' tools into their practices. From this, *Search for Mother* developed its' own momentum and became *Honored Birth*, a Natural Therapies in Birthing Program, credited with the Australian College of Midwifery.

But what to do, where to go, with the unearthed "mother" questions, sentiments, beliefs and expectations? How to "puzzle out" the persistent emergence of her complexities and the apparent dichotomies of her - all of which birthing people, non-birthing people nd practitioners continued to voice? It was clear that "fathoming mother" faced many. The way forward care-fully wrote itself into this companion *Search for Mother Journaling*.

Search for Mother Journaling offers a structure and a process for "fathoming mother". The structure is through organizing her into Mothers of Origin, the forms in which we encounter her in our lives; and into Mothers of Power, the intrinsic natures and essences of her which we have come into contact with, or not. Mothers of Origin and Mothers of Power are inter-dependent, each with wisdoms and frailties. The process is through reflecting, diarizing, accounting for and updating thinking and attitudes about mother.

I believe that linking with our Mothers of Origin, our Mothers of Power and their polarity deepens both our knowledge of her and our awareness of the resources we carry within to mother ourselves and others.

It is my hope that *Search for Mother Journaling* will bring an embrace for all your mother experiences both positive and negative; will enhance and inspire your innate mother-ness; and will embolden you and your children to know mothering from many.

Dedicated to and acknowledging
all who taught me about
mother and mothering:
The Mother within me
acknowledges the Mother within you.

Mothers of Origin

Usually, when we see the word mother, what comes to mind is biological mother: the woman who gave birth to us. However, as we live our lives we come to realize that we experience mother and mothering from many: adopting mothers, surrogate mothers, significant family and friends, inspirational work mentors, health healers and mother-nature. There are also biblical, spiritual and mythological mothers who might inspire us, such as Mother Mary, Mother Teresa, and in Greek mythos, Demeter, mother of Persephone. Then there are cultural mothers personified in the Mother Country concept. In due course I came to know the presence of one more: the Inside Mother.

I'd like to present the following mothers of origin and invite you to journal with them.

Biological Mother
Significant Mothers
Community and Organization Mothers
Cultural Mothers
Mythological, Spiritual, Biblical, Divine, Church Mothers
Earth Mother
Inside Mother

Biological Mother

Biological mother is she who conceived and birthed us, she who gave us our origin and our beginning. This role has become a little blurred with the reality of the surrogate mother, who has taken on producing a child who arrives through her body as a result of another's desire to conceive, birth, and provide origin for a child. If this is the case for you, for the purpose of simplifying your journaling, please consider biological mother as the woman who desired to conceive, to give birth to, and to provide origin for you.

Journaling with Biological Mother:

1. Write the attributes of your biological mother in the areas of:

Physical	
Name, Age, Place of Birth	
Appearance	
Voice, language, "sayings"	
Occupation	
Hobbies	
Passions	
Other	
Mental	
Education	
Career	
Employment	
Intellectual Interests – books, culture, music, theatre, movies	
Other	

Social	
Activities	
People	
Organizations	
Other	
Emotional	
Disposition	
Positive	
Negative	
Quirkiness	
Other	
Spiritual	
Beliefs	
Influences	
Attitudes	
Other	

2. From this character sketch write what you have taken, consciously and unconsciously into who you are:

3. Write what you have decided not to take into who you are:

4. Now list the attributes you have decided to maintain and next to each write a practical way you could bring this to your mothering:

These attributes and ways of bringing them to your mothering are your mother powers from your Biological Mother of Origin.

My Journaling with Biological Mother.

As I reflect on my time with my biological mother, fifty-four years, I remember with poignancy, these words I said at her funeral: "We are who we are because of who you were". However, I didn't know I carried so much of who she was until life events raised the question, "How did I survive that?" The answer is because of my mother's resilience. Whether it was genetic or experientially learnt is not the point here. My mother was monumentally resilient, I am, and now I heart-fully watch my daughters being so in their challenging young lives. Resilience or strength is a mother Power we explore more in the second section.

Conversely, I would have to say, a lot of who I am is because of who my mother wasn't and who I wanted her to be. For example, my mothers' interests and decisions revolved around my father. Although I know that this was a cultural and era norm, its impact is that I purposefully create my life with what I enjoy and am passionate about, both within and outside my family, and have urged my children to do the same.

The mother powers of strength and creation were gifted to me by my biological mother of origin from her arena of wisdoms and frailties.

Significant Mothers

The meaning of significant as important, critical, momentous and vital, and of mother as having many essences, powers and forms directs us to significant people who have been mother in our lives - be it adopted mother, foster mother, grandmother, godmother, aunt, sister, cousin, friend, a friend's mother, a neighbor, or a mentor; be it a male or a female; be it for extended or brief periods of our lives. Whether from conscious or unconscious words or actions, significant mothers have shaped who we are in our inner and outer worlds.

Journaling with a Significant Mother:

1. Write the attributes of a significant mother in the areas of:

Physical	
Name, Age, Place of Birth	
Appearance	
Voice, language, "sayings"	
Occupation	
Hobbies	
Passions	
Other	
Mental	
Education	
Career	
Employment	
Intellectual Interests – books, culture, music, theatre, movies	
Other	

Social	
Activities	
People	
Organizations	
Other	
Emotional	
Disposition	
Positive	
Negative	
Quirkiness	
Other	
Spiritual	
Beliefs	
Influences	
Attitudes	
Other	

2. From this character sketch write what you have taken consciously and unconsciously into who you are:

3. Write what you have decided not to take into who you are:

4. Now list the attributes you have decided on and next to each write a practical way to bring this to your mothering. For example, one of my significant mothers showed me the treasure of empathetic listening. To bring this into my mothering I mindfully decided, that when my children are talking, I will listen without interrupting, acknowledge, and then ask if they want a suggestion. I'm still practicing!

These attributes and ways of bringing them to your mothering are your mother powers from your significant mother of origin.

My Journaling with a Significant Mother.

Here I will choose an aunt. From her, I learnt unconditional acceptance and what it feels like to be listened to, no matter what my experiences and choices had been. I learnt there is always something in everyone's story that can be positively acknowledged, that judgment can be left out and that advice and "fixing" are not needed in order to feel listened to. She taught these things by showering me with them.

This aunt also exposed the substance required to honor personal boundaries and the imperative place of compassionate self-love and self-care in one's life. She did this by struggling to have her own boundaries and by not having adequate compassionate self-love and self-care.

Of course we must recognize our own predispositions and external influences in these matters. For her and for me, these are our generous natures and our strict, righteous, "others first" Baptist upbringings.

Now, as my aunt's sunset beckons, I listen to her and apply the gentle acceptance and acknowledgement with which she equipped me. We have become significant mothers for each other through the acceptance mother power.

Community and Organization Mothers

Community: society in a city, town or village[1]

Organization: a body of people united with collective purpose[2]

We are all part of, have been part of, and have had experiences with communities and organizations. Hopefully, some delivered "mothering" through nurturing, providing, teaching, loyalty, connection, and other mother powers. For example, the organizations, clubs and youth movements we may have belonged to in our childhoods, such as the scouting, YWCA, drama, music and public-speaking clubs were "mothers" through being teachers of skills. At school fetes, Rotary and Lion Clubs were "mother providers" through supplying food stalls which gave us nourishment and jumping castles and merry-go-rounds which gave us fun. Our councils and community committees also effect the mother essence of provider through implementing safe structures in parks, footpaths and shopping centres.

In theory, the organizations we work for are "mother providers" by disbursing salaries which bring sustenance. Generally, employers offer skill enhancement, mentoring, and professional development, thus taking on the mother role of teacher. Through organizing team and social activities, they extend the mother power of belonging and connection. In recent times protection procedures have been established through Occupational Health and Safety Regulations, and loyalty shown by provision of maternal and paternal leave and child care in workplaces. All these are mother traits. The organizations and committees we choose to be part of in our adult

---

[1]   Oxford Dictionary
[2]   Oxford Dictionary

lives "mother" by bonding us to our community. And finally, our health care system and its workers, in principle, provide "mothering" care and comfort.

Journaling with Community & Organization Mothers:

1. Reflect on and list from childhood to the present the communities and organizations you have been part of:

2. Reflect on and list what skills you gained from these communities and organizations. Then write a practical way to bring each skill into your mothering:

3. Reflect on and list what attributes and attitudes you gained from these communities and organizations and then a practical way to bring each into your mothering:

These skills, attributes, attitudes and ways to bring them to your mothering are your mother powers from your community and organization mothers of origin. They not only assist you to mother your own, but also nurture work, colleague, neighbourhood, and community relationships.

My Mother Journaling with Community and Organization:

One "mother" health organization I have had the privilege of being associated with is Mercy Gilbert Hospital in Arizona. Here, the commitment to whole- patient experience and excellence is realized through the Radical Loving Care Philosophy which espouses creating a healing culture to nurture both personnel and patients. This philosophy is based on the ancient tradition that love is at the centre of healing. At Mercy Gilbert Hospital this is put into practice, by, for example, employees being invited to have their hands blessed before their shifts. Further, at the entrance to each room is a hand plaque with the words "pause, reflect, heal" reminding staff of the healing in their hands and the purpose of their profession. The hospital gardens are designed into walking paths in the shape of infinity symbols, evoking in patients, visitors, and the workforce, that loving care is infinite. It's no wonder Mercy Gilbert Hospital has an employment waiting list! This is an exceptional example of an organization – a mother of origin, extending nurture – a mother of power. My short time at Mercy Gilbert Hospital has enthused me to propose the Radical Loving Care philosophy to Australian employers and organizations.

Another remarkable example of an organization "mothering" was through the nurse unit manager of midwifery at Mona Vale Hospital in Sydney. She invited me to teach birthing yoga within her unit and became my ardent mentor and supporter. The program grew to include endorsement by the whole unit, hospital, and the Northern New South Wales Health Area, and then further, to include birthing massage, yoga and massage therapy for staff, natural therapy education, retreats, post-natal yoga, women's groups for mothers and babies, a research project, and my book *Search for Mother*. This woman was a nurturing visionary, who facilitated my passion for equality and holistic health care. After her recent passing the unit was re-named and dedicated to her.

I will always be humbled by and grateful to these organizations for the mothering they poured into my work.

To conclude this section, I want to share this profound story which began at Mona Vale Hospital. It concerns a group of four women who attended my pre-natal yoga classes during their first, second and third pregnancies. These women have maintained their friendship, supported each other, and met (with their children) over the ensuing ten years as well as generously giving interviews in *Search for Mother*. One is now a yoga teacher and another has her own natural therapy business. When I'm in Sydney we all get together, including children, and mothering goes around our little community.

Cultural Mother Country

Culture: Humanism, a civilization involving upbringing, education, and learning.[3]

Cultural mother country can be defined as the country of our ancestral language. The label personifies culture and country into an icon of what it means to be a mother to society and to a nation. Mother culture represents an ideology which affords the mother powers of connection, protection and security. We generally choose to live in such a country and/or culture.

It's easy, in western, relatively peaceful, democratic situations, to take our cultural mother country lightly, that is, until we move into mothering and begin to consider the life we hope for, for our children.

Journaling with Cultural Mother:

1.   What is your mother culture country?

_____

Oxford Dictionary

2. Why have you chosen, or chosen to stay in this mother culture country?

3. Take one reason you have chosen your mother culture country and write a practical way you could bring this to your mothering. For example, one reason I believe Australia is a good choice for my children is because of the opportunities to live and work in environments where integrity and equality are core values. It's always been fundamental to me that my children, myself, and in fact, all peoples, experience fair-ness and equality. This has played out, for example, in our scrabble and monopoly games from childhood right through to adulthood where we all ensure that everyone has equal turns.

The reasons you have identified above are your mother powers to provide a cultural mother country for your children.

My Journaling with Cultural Mother Country – Australia.

My parents emigrated from Sri Lanka, then Ceylon, in 1956, as it loosened itself from the Commonwealth. They did so for protection, security and to build an abundant life in which to raise a family. They arrived with two metal trunks, one hundred pounds, one friend already here, and me on the way. Eventually, both my mothers' and my fathers' families emigrated and an abundant life was made for my three brothers and myself. However, along the way to this abundant life, my parents felt understandable loss and sadness at the disintegration of the mother country, culture, and society in which they grew up. Additionally, they were faced with the challenges of creating connection in their new mother country. Of course there was also gratitude and relief for the profusion of prospects available here. Unhappily, I inherited this range of feelings which were compounded by the following: I was dark skinned and had curries for lunch at school while others had vegemite and peanut butter sandwiches; my home was full of artifacts and pictures from Sri Lanka and we were constantly visited by other dark skinned people who spoke another language. These feelings of difference and disconnection from where I was being brought up, persisted well into my adult life and resulted in my travelling, living and working in many countries around the world. Perhaps I was unconsciously seeking connection, home and belonging. As my children arrived and grew, I could clearly see that the opportunities and freedoms Australia has, would proffer an abundant life for them, so there was no impetus to relocate.

In spite of this, the sense of Australia being a mother culture for me only arose as I began to work in remote and rural Aboriginal communities. I fell in love with the land and was nurtured by the wisdom teachings of its Indigenous people.

Belonging came through being in the awesome beauty and vastness of outback Australia, through learning of its Indigenous culture, and by working in Aboriginal health. It came through the Mother Powers – Creation, Connection and Wisdom Teaching. I'll finish here by sharing that this understanding and acceptance of my mother country being Australia happened through writing this mother journaling process.

Mythological Biblical Spiritual Mothers

Myth: Fable parable allegory tradition legend[4]

Biblical: Based on the bible[5]

Spiritual – sacred unearthly unworldly holy supernatural ethereal divine godlike celestial heavenly transcendent related to church and places of worship[6]

Whatever your take on life and its grand questions, there are mothers in mythology, mothers in sacred texts and mothers who speak to us through ethereal and supernatural means and dreams.

As I researched the biblical slant on mother and mothering I unearthed the word mother in the Bible three hundred times. Psalm 113:9 states: "Mothers are a "gift of God". Some notable Biblical mothers are Mother Mary, with the Mother Power of Acceptance; Ruth, who said to her daughter in law, "Your people are my people" thereby extending the Mother Power of Connection; and Mrs. Noah, documented by some as the mother of animals giving to them the Mother Power of Nurture.

In England, the church is historically regarded as a mother. People who visit the church of their baptism are said to have gone "a-mothering", while Cathedrals are referred to as "Mother Church". Some of the mother roles churches of any religion profess to offer are: nurturer, carer, comforter, offerer of shelter and sustenance, teacher, and forgiver. People continue to seek succour from the church in

---

4   Oxford Dictionary
5   Oxford Dictionary
6   Oxford Dictionary

times of need, of sorrow, loss, and confusion, as well as in times of celebration. The church cares and provides for the homeless, the needy, the sick and the dying. All these are essences of mother.

Spiritual mothers who inspire me are: Joan of Arc from medieval times who fought for equality and human rights till her death at the stake; Florence Nightingale, a nurse in the Crimean War who kept a lamp alight day and night while tending the wounded; Mary McKillop, the first Australian saint who set up countless homes for abandoned children; and Mother Teresa. Mother Teresa, on receiving her Nobel Peace Prize in 1979 was asked "What can we do to promote world peace?" to which she replied, "Go home and love your family". The books *Women of Power and Grace* by Timothy Conway and *Women Who Run with the Wolves* by Clarissa Pinkenbar burst with biographies and teachings of spiritual divine mothers.

Then there are mothers in fairy tales who wave magic wands both positive and negative; and mythological mothers who offer us rich tapestries of other worlds and deities. Some who have taught me are:

Demeter- Greek Goddess of Harvest whose daughter Persephone, was abducted by Hades, King of the Underworld and forced to marry him. Demeter followed her daughter to the Underworld, risking her own life, defying the laws of the seasons, pleading with Hades, and eventually bargaining with the seasons themselves to release Persephone.

Haumea - Polynesian Goddess of Child Birth who taught women how to give birth by pushing their baby out between their legs. Folklore tells that prior to this babies were cut from the womb – fascinating when the trends and cycles in caesarean birthing are considered.

Rennet - Egyptian Goddess of Breast Feeding and Soul Names is said to be responsible for creating the baby's desire to feed from its' mothers' breasts. Rennet also taught new mothers their baby's soul name, a soul name being that which protects and holds the framework for personality.

Heqet - Egyptian Fertility Goddess who trained women as midwives.

Sar-Akka - from Scandinavia who helped open the womb of women in birthing.

Mawu - African Mother Goddess - in this mythology the Great Earth Mother, is a black woman Mawu, meaning Mother of us all. Her fiery, dark, labyrinth earth womb is believed to be the place of entry into this world and the place of return where we await rebirth.

So we see that mythological spiritual mothers are present in countries and cultures around the world and throughout history, exemplifying that the search to connect with, and have an understanding about mother is universal and spiritual.

What can be made of all this?

Perhaps it reminds us that Mothers of Origin are both tangible and intangible. That they are embodied in biological and mysterious spiritual forms, all beseeching us to accept their wisdoms, frailties and Mother Powers through not only physical experiences, but also through parable, fable and miracle. Perhaps mother always has, and always will, retain an element of mystery, of conundrum and puzzle. Perhaps she is meant to - for if we could decode mothering completely we may leap far and fast and away from the sometimes seemingly impossible and insurmountable tasks of mother love we are called upon to give.

And lastly, I surmise that mother truly is a reflection of mystery, parallel with the mystery that is God.

Journaling with Mythological Biblical Spiritual Divine Church Mother:

1. What are some of your mystical mother favorites?

2. Why are you drawn to these mothers?

3. Take one reason from Q 2 and write a practical way you could bring this to your mothering. For example, I am very drawn to Demeter Mother of Persephone because of the strength she showed in fighting the underworld for the return of her daughter. Whether myth, fact or mythological fact, Demeter has given me strength and perseverance when dealing with the underworld of the health issues of my children and my mother.

These reasons and the ways to bring them to your mothering are your mother powers from your mythological spiritual mothers of origin. They augment how you mother those whom you love.

Mother Earth

Her awesome grandness, her majestic silence and songs, her stillness and her wildness have long brought nurturing and renewal. This "mother" grows food and circulates oxygen but she sustains so much more than our physical body. She is also the mother who nourishes our spiritual eyes through beauty, our spiritual ears with animal and weather music, our spiritual noses with evocative fragrances, and our spiritual nervous system and cells with cool breeze, pure air, fresh raindrops and the warmth of fire.

A delightful way to interact with Mother Earth's immeasurable beauty and her creative power of life, death, rebirth and immortality is to walk the circles of a nature maze or labyrinth.

Journaling with Mother Nature:

1. Recall a nature place which has nurtured you:

2. Through which senses do you receive mother nature nurturer here?

3. When you commune with Mother Nature what happens in your Physical body:

Mind:

Emotions:

Spirit:

4. Take some of these responses and write practical ways you could bring these to you mothering. For example, leaning my back against a tree calms and quiets me so when my children were young and needed "time out" I sat them with their back against a tree.

These physical, mental, emotional and spiritual responses and ways of bringing them to your mothering are your nature mother of origin powers to employ with those whom you mother.

My Journaling with Mother Nature.

From the sand and rocks of beach and desert on my feet, I am warmed and reminded of the cavernous depths of the earth to which I am connected, and that softness and roughness are beauty.

From the trees, their strength, girth, height, and their smooth rough bark on my spine, I become taller, straighter, stronger, reminded of my purpose.

From the endless earth's curvature and horizon, I become still in body and mind, and calm in emotion.

From all the colors painted on sky and earth, my vision is replete.

From the oceans, rivers, waterfalls and lakes, my spirit becomes clean and restored.

When my children were young we went on camping road trips every school holiday. These times were about beauty and simple connection to family and nature. Being in nature is as vital a nurturer for me now as it was then.

The Inside Mother

The Inside Mother lives by many names: Higher Self, Intuition and the Knowing that knows without knowing how it knows. She dwells inside our depths, waiting with her well of wisdom from all our mothers of origin and all our mothers of power. Waiting for us to hear her language, her whisperings, her mantras, her hymns. Waiting for us to call her, to consult her, to know her comfort.

Journaling with Your Inside Mother:

1. What are your words for Inside Mother?

2. How do you connect/ listen to your Inside Mother?
   (For example, gut feelings, meditation, a consistent word in your head, a body sensation)

3. What are some of the things your inside mother advises/tells/ shows you to do?

4. Which of these are
   Easy:

   Difficult:

5. Take one that you find difficult and one that you find easy and write a practical way to bring these to your mothering. For example, my inside mother tells me to care for my physical health through food that suits my body. This is challenging for me because of my busy life so I translate it into my mothering by having a vegetable garden with my children.

Remembering your Inside Mother, listening to her, and following her guidance is your mother power from this mother of origin. She helps you to give and to receive mothering.

My Journaling with My Inside Mother.

This began anew and resolutely when my daughters became teenagers. For it was then that I clearly and distressingly began to see my life challenges of boundaries, nurturing myself and making meaningful connection with my mother playing out in my relationships with them and in their relationships in their outside worlds. This eye opener led to more soul searching, guilt trips, attempts at self-forgiveness and self-acceptance, further self-help book reading, plentiful discussion with friends, and some discussion with counsellors.

What eventually became key, was listening to my body.

This might sound incredible as I had been teaching yoga for over ten years and yoga is about listening to your body. The change that transformed was, that whenever I detected any anxiety, stress, or discomfort in my body, I now gave it the voice of my Inside Mother: my protector, my nurturer, my wisdom teacher. I identified these body perceptions as her signals of communication to me, just as unborn babies communicate with their mother through body messages of stretching, kicking and moving around.

Next I frustratingly attempted to interpret the meaning of these body messages with the human means of words and concepts.

Finally I painstakingly comprehended that in order to receive what my inside mother-intuition-knowing was telling or showing

I simply needed to be still and to be still with my daughters.

Mothers of Power

The concept of many essences of Mother is presented in Jamie Sam's *Thirteen Mothers of Wisdom* and is based on Native American Indian tradition. Her exposition affirms for me that there are power essences of mother which define her and that are universally experienced. In this section I set out to unravel and describe both the positives and the negatives of these essences which I have named mothers of power.

Hopefully, our positive experiences of mother fill us with enhanced self confidence, self esteem and the desire to channel, emulate and bestow similar positive experiences and feelings, augmented with our own unique mother-ness, to those we care for.

Our seemingly negative mother experiences that we strive to discard and not to emulate are equally or more important to acknowledge and move forward from so that we can mother free from anger, hurt, resentment, guilt and complexity. So that our feelings, desires and the ways we mother, are in alignment with our love for those who have come to us through family.

These are the mothers of power I have consistently identified throughout my time as mother and daughter and which have been shared with me by many:

Unconditional love
Acceptance
Strength
Forgiveness
Loyalty
Connection
Creator
Protector
Wisdom Teacher.

I invite you to Journal with
mothers of power.
Reflect and write what comes to you
in whatever order and sections you
are drawn to. Each mother of power
offers an accompanying meditation.

Unconditional Love

These two words together conjure up a love that gives the impression of being at the pinnacle of all love, whether the love be Divine or Human. Being on this pinnacle unconditional love can both dazzle and set up for crushing disappointment. Whatever its basis, from Christ to New-Age, from myth to grounded theory, unconditional love seems one of the more profound intangibles of mother.

Dr. McGarey, my colleague, known as the Mother of Holistic Medicine in America, said when talking with me about *Search for Mother*, "It is my experience that God has established laws and perhaps the law of unconditional love is manifested in the action of love from mother to child".

My qualitative research showed the following beliefs and experiences around unconditional love: mothers intently aspire to give unconditional love; we come into this world head-strongly believing that unconditional love is our birthright from mother; mothers should know how to "do" unconditional love; and, that as life happens, few have escaped disillusionment from those they believed to be able and available to offer unconditional love.

When we experience unconditional love we feel love that is unqualified, unrestricted, absolute, pure, complete, actual, authoritative, perfect, entire, ultimate, eternal, and ever-lasting.

When we experience love that is not unconditional we are subject to conditional affection and praise, comparative praise, qualified praise, contingencies, being accountable, feeling dependant.

Journaling with Unconditional Love:

Your words for Unconditional Love: (please use any from the list above)

Check from which Mothers of Origin you have experienced Unconditional Love:

Biological Mother	
Significant Women or Men	
Community Organization Health Care	
Culture	
Mythological Spiritual Divine Church Mother Beings	
Mother Earth	
Your Inside Mother	
Other	

1. Take one unconditional love experience from the list above. Image and write, for example, a place, time, interaction, conversation:

Complete with "I felt unconditional love when I/he/she did/said………."

2. Take an experience when you did not feel unconditionally loved. Image and Write:

3. Write how you would have liked this experience to be, in other words, rewrite that history:

4. What is it in the rewritten story that brings you to feel unconditionally loved?

5. Consider something that gives you a feeling of unconditional love and write a practical way to bring this to your mothering:

Identifying what brings you unconditional love and ways to bring this to your mothering is your resource from your unconditional love mother power.

Unconditional Love Meditation Ceremony:

Effect your unconditional love ceremony either in nature or with images of nature around you such as green candles, flowers, herbs, photos of your favorite places.

Rest easy. Breathe easy. Personality at ease. Thinking at ease.

Image yourself on grass. Under a blue, blue sky. With clouds scattering pictures above you and breeze and sun on your skin. At first your eyes are open to see beauty. Then gently you close them to feel the sun and the breeze on your eyelids. Birds are singing. Flowers waft freshness. In this moment, you know that all is beauty. That you are beauty, and that this knowing of yourself as beauty is unconditional love.

As you commune with the mother power of unconditional love observe that you feel loved. Self-praise blazes with your perfection. There is no need for you to defend, explain, and account for yourself, your actions, or your beliefs. From here you can nurture your unconditional love for yourself. And from here you can offer others unconditional love.

My Journaling with Unconditional Love.

Reviewing those I believed were always able, always available, and from whom I had an expectation of unconditional love, has often left me wondering if my understanding of it is completely incorrect, if it really exists and if it is really possible to love unconditionally. There was one time when my mother responded to my barrage of adolescent rudeness by hanging up the phone as we spoke. She only did that once, but that once was the time I questioned whether perhaps she'd stopped loving me.

We all have our limits and boundaries and it is important for us to have them. Does this mean when a person does not seem to "be there" for us they have stopped loving us? My slow and painful conclusion about this is that in a moment when a person appears to not "be there" unreservedly for us, they are actually practicing unconditional love for themselves by honoring their own boundaries.

I learnt that it is at this precise moment that we must summon the mother power of unconditional love for ourselves.

Acceptance

We have all experienced both acceptance and non-acceptance from our mothers of origin.

Acceptance for you may arrive from a geographical location – a mother country, town or dwelling. Or mother nature's homes of trees and skies and seas and birds. Or from a mother person who knows the who and how and why of you. Or when you listen to the calm voice of your inside mother. Or other sources of acceptance that you alone discover.

When we feel acceptance we feel approval, affirmation, validation and being received as adequate, true and favorable. Acceptance feels safe. Feels being just right, appreciated, prized, treasured, valued, cherished, believed in. Acceptance is like arriving home.

When we do not feel acceptance, we experience judgment, criticism, being "not good enough", being compared to familial, cultural and other/s or your own standards, achievements, ways of being, and benchmarks. We feel ostracism, favoritism, being ignored, rejected.

Journaling with Acceptance:

Your Words for Acceptance:

Check from which Mothers of Origin you have experienced Acceptance:

Biological Mother	
Significant Women or Men	
Community Organization Health Care	
Culture	
Mythological Spiritual Divine Church Mother Beings	
Mother Earth	
Your Inside Mother	
Other	

1. Take one acceptance experience from the list above. Image and write this. For example, place, time, interaction, conversation:

Complete with "I felt accepted when I/he/she did/said........."

2. Take an experience when you did not feel accepted. Image and write:

Complete with "I didn't feel accepted when I/he/she did/said......:

3. Re-vision and write how you would have liked this experience to be, in other words, rewrite that history:

4. What is it in the rewritten story that brings you to feel acceptance?

5. Consider something that gives you a feeling of brings you acceptance and write a practical way you could bring this to your mothering:

Identifying what brings you acceptance and ways to bring this to your mothering is your resource from your acceptance mother of power.

Acceptance Meditation Ceremony:

Affect your acceptance ceremony space with roses, pictures of roses or essence of rose and a pink candle. Wearing something pink is wonderful. Placing a pink rose on your heart is also wonderful, pink being the yogic colour of acceptance and love.

Lie comfortably on your back, resting. Allow your torso to become soft. Front and back. Feel the place of your heart which may not necessarily be where your physical heart is but perhaps where you feel from. Begin to breathe in through the front of your heart, imagining the perfume of pink roses. Sense the rose perfume entering through the front of your heart, into your heart center and then leaving your heart through your back. Then sense fresh rose perfume entering your back into your heart and out through the front of your heart. Breathe the soft, pink rose perfume of acceptance into, and out of, your heart. In and out. Until your heart has become the most spectacular blossoming rose you've ever seen. This is the Rose of Acceptance. Its perfume wafts around you, encircling, encompassing, up and over, down and under, through all of who you are and all of who you long to be.

Acceptance lives in this rose in your heart. It perfumes the wearying droughts of insecurity, fear of failure, feeling less than, feeling self-discontent. Of the defeats of trying and trying and trying.

Here in the rose of your heart you are home. Here you belong. Here is a place of quietness and confidence and security where you are known and understood. Here yearning is soothed. Here you are accepted.

Valerie Albrecht

My Journaling with Acceptance

Here I'll share one of my friends. We've been friends for about ten years, have a deep philosophical and spiritual connection and have worked together in my Natural Healing Center. As we now don't live in the same city we only see and speak to each other a few times a year. Whenever we speak however, she is totally present with my stories and whatever is confronting me. She has never criticized or judged my decisions, actions or the outcomes they brought. She seems to offer the exact words and suggestions I need in that moment. She also seems to be going away whenever I need a respite and so offers her home – and her dog to mind. How does a person know how to give such acceptance? Through experiencing and receiving it? Through carrying the genes of it? Through learning and practicing it with determined discipline, intention and focus? Through some sort of Divine channeling? I asked her once and she said she didn't know she was as skilled with giving acceptance as I thought she was and thanked me sincerely for the observation.

My upcoming book, *The Story Behind the Story,* is of a Navajo Medicine Man, a paraplegic who grew up between two worlds: western medicine rehabilitation and traditional Navajo medicine and teachings. *The Story Behind the Story* is one of Acceptance. How it came to me is another story. Why it came to me was to teach self-acceptance. Self-acceptance has been one of my greatest challenges and Medicine Man one of my greatest teachers.

Which brings us back to the question of how to do acceptance. Over the years I've dissected acceptance into the following components: self-approval, self-belief, self-appreciation, self-care, self-listening, self-forgiveness and self-blessing. I apply this by writing each day something about myself from each component e.g. self-belief: Today I believe in myself to get that chapter finished; self-blessing: Today

I bless myself with sun on my back while I work etc. This discipline has resulted in a remarkable metamorphosis of my self acceptance. The stronger and more consistent I'm becoming with accepting all of myself, the more effective I find I am at giving out the mother power of acceptance to others.

Strength

Strength: courage, resilience, fortitude, forbearance, resolute power, might, toughness, durability, vigor, soundness, unwavering focus on what the outcome needs to be – these are what makes strength happen. Strength both arises from and brings determination.

When we do not experience mother strength, we feel a certain lack of stability, of soundness, of grounded-ness in our home, in our relationship with mother, with others and with ourselves. We begin to carry a "precipice" feeling in our lives. Our ideal, our expectation of mother strength fractures, and instead, a perception of frailty, of feebleness, of a lack of her personal power and ours, surfaces.

Journaling with Strength:

Your words for Strength:

Check from which Mothers of Origin you have experienced Strength:

Biological Mother	
Significant Women or Men	
Community Organization Health Care	
Culture	
Mythological Spiritual Divine Church Mother Beings	
Mother Earth	
Your Inside Mother	
Other	

1. Take one experience of mother strength. Image and write. For example, place, time, interaction, conversation:

Complete with "I felt mother strength when I/he/she did/said………."

2. Take an experience when you did not feel mother strength. Image and write:

3. Write how you would have liked this experience to be, in other words, rewrite that history:

4. What is it in the rewritten story that brings you to feel strength from another?

5. Consider something that brings you a feeling of strength and write a practical way to bring this to your mothering:

Identifying what brings you strength and ways to bring this to your mothering is your resource from your strength mother of power.

Strength Meditation and Ceremony:

Effect by visualizing your breath throughout this meditation as soft, white mist gradually transforming into sunbeams, then, to a solid beam of golden light.

Breathing easy. Breathing easy. Breathing soft white mist.

Breathing easy. Breathing easy. Breathing sunbeams.

Breathing easy. Breathing easy. Breathing a beam of light.

Breathing to your toes, feet, legs, pelvis.

Breathing to your fingers, hands, arms, shoulders.

Breathing to your torso front and back.

Breathing up your spine to your neck.

Breathing to your chin, cheeks, jaw, nose, eyes, eyebrows, forehead, scalp, hair. Breathing easy. Breathing easy.

Breathing to your kidneys, liver, spleen, gallbladder, pancreas, your lungs, diaphragm, heart, thyroid, parathyroid, pituitary, pineal gland.

Breathing to the organs of sense on your face, your skin, and your brain.

Breathing soft white mist.

Breathing sunbeams.

Breathing a solid beam of golden strength.

Valerie Albrecht

My Journaling with Strength

When my mother left her family, her country, her culture to make a new life in Australia; when our family relocated to another state because of my father's career, and then again a few years later to another state for another career; when she battled cancer, and when she observed her children fraught and broken hearted in their lives, I asked myself, "How did she survive?"

When my marriage ended after twenty two years; when I lost significant money in a business; when I made poor choices in love; when my children turned adolescent fury against me; and when they and I suffered serious illness all in the same year I asked myself, "How did we survive?"

When I chose time out to write each book enduring the consequent monetary stress; when no one understood why I left stable jobs to travel and research; and when I kept stepping out of expected family life styles which brought on well-meaning inquisitions from those nearest and dearest, I asked myself, "How did I survive?"

When I couldn't understand why so many challenges and dualities accompanied my believing in, and following my passions; when open doors beckoned and then without warning slammed; when the way I had made sense of things didn't seem to make sense anymore, and when I wept with despair and yet did not give up I asked, "How am I still surviving?"

When I watched my eldest daughter not give up with her recovery over five years and when I saw the other one not give up on her career in fashion which kept her financially struggling I asked, "How did they survive?"

Then I knew:

My strength and their strength comes from the strength of my biological mother of origin.

Forgiveness

Positive Experience: to pardon, excuse, exonerate, clear, pardon, waive, to feel health and breathe fresh.

Negative Experience: to feel blamed, resented, accused, censured, be-littled, to have a grudge held against you, to have something thrown in your face, to feel vindictiveness, hard heartedness, and an absence of compassion.

Journaling with Forgiveness:

This may feel overwhelming and not possible. My mother journaling with forgiveness has many, many times rendered me as I relived my actions and those of others. I suggest that you begin with experiences which are less formidable which will allow you to re-feel.

Your words for Forgiveness:

Check from which Mothers of Origin you have experienced Forgiveness:

Biological Mother	
Significant Women or Men	
Community Organization Health Care	
Culture	
Mythological Spiritual Divine Church Mother Beings	
Mother Earth	

Your Inside Mother	
Other	

1. Take one experience of forgiveness. Image and write. For example, place, time, interaction, conversation:

Complete with "I felt forgiveness when I/he/she did/said.........."

2. Take an experience when you did not feel forgiveness. Image and write:

3. Write how you would have liked this experience to be, in other words, rewrite that history:

4. What is it in the rewritten story that brings you to feel forgiveness?

5. Consider something that brings you a feeling of forgiveness. Write a practical way to bring this to your mothering:

Identifying what brings you to feel forgiveness and ways to bring this to your mothering is your resource from your forgiveness mother of power.

Forgiveness Meditation Ceremony:

Affect by writing on pieces of paper:

"I am no longer willing to carry the pain my/your/person's name action/words of .... have caused me. I did my best with who I was at the time. I forgive myself/you."

Continue with as many situations and people as you can at this time.

Lie comfortably. Warmly. Image yourself as a white dove flying higher and higher. Far and higher. Far and higher. From the dove's wings see the pieces of paper you've just written on fluttering, off. Fluttering. Fluttering away. Smaller and smaller. Evaporating. Disappearing. Vanishing.

As you are ready, sit up and dispose of the papers however it seems right for you – in the rubbish, burning, burying, or in the bottom of a drawer or box. Sense relief. Sense lightness. Sense forgiveness.

Valerie Albrecht

My Journaling with Forgiveness

Forgiveness is when I sit with all of myself.

And know

I don't mean to ever do any less

Than my Best -

Which is not always how things I do

Turn out.

Forgiveness is saying

That I did my best with who I was at the time,

And reassuring

The who I am now

That I have learnt from those experiences.

Forgiveness happens

Even though I may not feel

Immediately

Better.

Loyalty

Loyalty is being true and self-less to who you are. Acting in accordance with who you are, and your beliefs. Making choices cognizant and of integrity with your essence, your uniqueness. Your gifts. Your purpose. Your drive. Your passions. Being true enough to yourself to disappoint another, to risk dismantling another's perception of you for who you know you are. Being true enough to yourself to admit to others that some of your choices and their outcomes have caused you heartache, cost you money, cost you face, hurt your pride, momentarily slipped you from your own self esteem.

Loyalty is earnest faithful devoted dependable true.

Positive experiences of loyalty bring contentment, self-security, self-acceptance, steadfastness, grace, dignity, honor, fairness, allegiance.

Negative experiences of loyalty bring detachment disconnectedness falseness Self-sacrifice and often deceit and untruth.

Journaling with Loyalty:

Your words for Loyalty:

Check from which Mothers of Origin you have experienced Loyalty.

Biological Mother	
Significant Women or Men	
Community Organization Health Care	
Culture	

Mythological Spiritual Divine Church Mother Beings	
Mother Earth	
Your Inside Mother	
Other	

1. Take one experience of Loyalty. Image and write. For example, place, time, interaction, conversation:

Complete with "I felt loyalty when I/he/she did/said........."

2. Take an experience when you did not feel loyalty. Image and write:

3. Write how you would have liked this experience to be, in other words, rewrite that history:

4. What is it in the rewritten story that brings you to feel loyalty?

5. Consider something that brings you a feeling of loyalty. Write a practical way of how to bring this to your mothering:

Identifying what brings you a sense of loyalty from yourself and others and ways to bring this to your mothering is your resource from your loyalty mother of power.

Loyalty Meditation and Ceremony:

Affect your ceremony space by creating a Circle of Loyalty around you with tea light candles. Connect the tea lights by weaving a web of ribbon, string or wool. Next to each candle place a photo or the name of a person who has shown you loyalty.

Sit or lie in the circle. Happy. Peaceful. Safe.

Send a prayer of gratitude to each person specifying how they have shown you loyalty. For example, thank you (name) for ....

Those who have not shown you loyalty may come to mind. Some of these may be those who have also shown you loyalty. That is, they were loyal and not, in different or even the same situations. That is, they did their best with who they were in each situation. Trust your intuition on whether to move these folks in or out of your circle. Do your best to ignore your judgment and criticism of your decisions. It is your Circle of Loyalty and its' purpose is to be your safe place.

When finished pause, reflect, revisit your circle. You might find you want to re-position people. Know that as you do, you are gaining more understanding, acceptance and forgiveness for your loyalty experiences.

My Journaling with Loyalty

My mother used to sign letters and cards to me with the words "love always". Looking back, the knowing that knows without knowing how it knows, knows that she always did. No matter how abominably awful and rebellious my adolescent behavior was toward her. No matter the year I wouldn't talk to her as I tried to process her. No matter how relentlessly and un-benevolently I took her apart when I had my own children, birthday cards with "love always" always arrived.

During my work in birthing and the writing of *Search for Mother*, understanding and compassion for her unexpectedly arose and I dedicated that book to: "my mother who never, ever gave up on me".

Now when I write to my children I sign off with "love always" because I will. No matter how abominably behaved they might be toward me. No matter that they stop talking to me as they take me apart trying to process me, the mother power of loyalty somehow finds a way to sign birthday cards with "love always".

Nowadays my birthday cards arrive from my father alone and they too are signed "love always".

Connection

Positive connection stitches us to our roots, predecessors, countries, umbilical cords, our history, our innermost self. Making connection is to link, relate, combine, associate, bond, and tie, to feel union and deep affinity with. Connection takes us to the heart of our self and our families, to the centre of our existence, to belonging, to our pasts and to our futures. Mothers are fundamental to connection.

One way of understanding connection is through reincarnation, the concept of souls as eternal. In this philosophy our souls begin shrouded in mystery and timelessness. Each soul is said to belong to a soul family, and have a mate or many with connection that is instantly felt as deep affinity, either positive or negative. This affinity is especially evident when mother and child souls embed during conception and pregnancy. Their connection is tangible through the physical umbilical cord, pulsating with blood, oxygen, and nutrition; and intangible, pulsating with feelings, dreams, and inexplicable dialogues during pregnancy. After birth, connection is cemented as mother tells stories, shows photos, and shares heirlooms. Then as family treasures are passed from one generation to the next, we come to see where we've been, why we've become who we've become, and where we may be going. We see ourselves in those we are connected to, whether we like what we see or not! Sometimes it is enough connection just to see that we are connected! The rebelliousness of adolescence can bring out the sharpest of shears to cut away our connections. But somehow in softer moments we are back, aching for the stories, hunting for the photo, securing the heirloom, because, somewhere inside us we know connection brings something to hold onto that will never break.

A lack of connection brings a sense of dislocation, of lostness, of searching, of void, vacuum, unbelonging, feelings of being adrift, bewildered, confused, of being pre-occupied with finding, with feeling, with pursuing............. connection

Journaling with Connection:

This can bring a crushing sense of sadness for those who have passed before we made and/or valued connection with them. It can also bring astonishing relief when we finally experience that we do belong somewhere.

Your words for Connection:

Check from which Mothers of Origin you have experienced Connection:

Biological Mother	
Significant Women or Men	
Community Organization Health Care	
Culture	
Mythological Spiritual Divine Church Mother Beings	
Mother Earth	
Your Inside Mother	
Other	

1. Choose one experience of feeling connection. Write its' story, its' time, place, feeling, conversation:

Complete with "I felt connection when I/he/she did/said........."

2. Take an experience when you did not feel connection. Image and write.

3. Write how you would have liked this experience to be, in other words, rewrite that history:

4. What is it in the rewritten story that brings you to feel connection?

5. Consider something that brings you a feeling of connection. Write a practical way you can bring connection to your mothering:

Identifying who and what bring you a sense of connection and ways to bring this to your mothering is your resource from your connection mother of power.

Connection Meditation and Ceremony:

In the centre of a largish piece of paper write your name in a circle. Draw lines radiating from your circle and a circle at the end of each connecting line. In each circle write a person's name or organization or any Mother of Origin with whom you have experienced connection. Then write in this circle your connection to this person e.g. Mother Ivy: I am daughter of Ivy. Grandmother Joan: I am granddaughter of Joan. If you write your Church or an organization follow with, for example, "I am valued member". You could also put photos of each in each circle.

When you have been as thorough as you can be for now, rest comfortably.

Breathe easy. Quiet your mind.

Place your palm on your belly button. Feel its hollow softness. Its effortless rising and falling. Feel the warmth shared from your hand to your belly button and the warmth returned from your belly button to your hand. Listen to the contented gurgling of your belly as you settle into relaxation.

Imagine yourself floating in an indigo night sky. Floating, floating amongst millions of stars glowing all around you. The night air is a perfect temperature. You are light and as ethereal as the stars you float by.

Imagine at your belly button, a ribbon umbilical cord, gently unfurling into this quiet night sky. Watch it beckoning from your belly button to a star. Observe it tenderly curling around and joining with this star. Notice this star smiling, becoming a face you recognize. It's a face of someone important to you, perhaps someone in one of your loyalty circles. Intuit connection with this person. Gaze on their face, listen to what they may be saying to you, feel how you feel being with them.

Now watch another ribbon gently unfurling out from your belly button, joining with another star. See this star smiling, becoming another face you recognize. Another someone who is important to you in some way – in childhood or later, at work, or someone who perhaps encouraged you in some way. Or perhaps someone simply passing by you in the street with just the perfect word. Intuit connection with this person.

Watch the ribbon again reaching to another star person and another and another. All have been or are important to you. Eventually you notice a web of ribbon has been woven from your belly button out into the night sky, joining you to those in the stars. You are in the centre. Intuit your place, your connection, your belonging with these who have come to you in this meditation.

My Journaling with Connection

Connection takes me from umbilical cord to umbilical cord. Back and back. To Mother Earth. Her roots. Her soil. Her Ground. Her Mud. To Trees. Trunks. Branches. Twigs. Buds. Leaves. Flowers. Back to a seed. I am from a seed. An embryonic seed. As was my mother, my grandmothers and my great grandmothers. Their seeds were planted in Ceylon and before that in Portugal and Holland. And long, long before that, way, way back in time, in the birth place of souls. Now I am a bringer of connection for my mob. They don't listen much yet – but they will. The murmuring of those gone before will call them. The footsteps of their ancestors will echo in their hallways. The who of who I am, will insist they ask me, "Where did you come from?"

Creation

Some say that to birth is the ultimate creation and that the person who births us is the ultimate creator whether we consider the "God" creator, the mother/father creator, the creator of works of art and literature, the architect, engineer, town planner, interior designer, landscaper or any creator of environments, businesses, homes and relationships. Anyone who creates anything of whatever magnitude is a creator creating, irrespective of the creation being harmonious or discordant. In this way of looking, we are all creators creating, and will continue to be so throughout our lives. Whether we subscribe to creation theories of religion, fate, re-incarnation, genetics or environment, we who birth anyone or anything are creators.

Regardless of all this though, mother, human and animal, remain the penultimate creators as they have fashioned and grown within their body another life.

Positive aspects: to formulate, fashion from, originate, produce, ordain, invent, beget, design, construct, or to innovate, which carries an element of mystery and ingenuity.

Negative aspects: to destroy, tear down, desicreate, nullify, void, disappear, take away, un-create, humiliate, impair, abolish, raze, devastate, demolish, flatten, wreck.

Journaling with Creator:

This is indeed interesting, as we consider what and who we and others have created and what our experience of these creations is.

Valerie Albrecht

Your words for Creator:

Check from which Mothers of Origin you have experienced Creation:

Biological Mother	
Significant Women or Men	
Community Organization Health Care	
Culture	
Mythological Spiritual Divine Church Mother Beings	
Mother Earth	
Your Inside Mother	
Other	

1. Choose one experience of creation – yours or anothers'. Write its story, time, place, feeling, conversation:

Complete with "I felt creation when I/he/she did/said.........."

2. Take an experience when you felt negative creation. For example, it could be something that a mother of origin tried to create with you which didn't work out; something that you tried to create which didn't turn out how you had envisioned - a business or personal goal or an interaction with someone; or a time when you received negative feedback for something you created which you thought was wonderful. Image and write:

3. Write how you would have liked this experience to be, in other words, rewrite that history:

4. What is it in the rewritten story that brings you a positive experience of creation?

5. Take a situation that brings you an experience of creation and write a practical way to bring this to your mothering:

Identifying what you and your mothers of origin have created, both positive and negative, and the feelings this brought you, is your resource from your creator mother of power.

Creator Meditation and Ceremony:

Affect your ceremony space with orange candles, flowers, crystals or whatever orange image or symbol you are drawn to – orange being the yogic chakra color of the second sacral energy centre of creation. It is the area around the belly button. Then take plenty of relaxed time to create a vision board of pictures and/or words representing your highest desired outcomes for your life in:

The physical sense: career, income, home, garden, community, travel, family, friendships.

The mental sense: education, intellectual pursuits, hobbies, interests, entertainment, cultures you desire to experience.

The emotional sense: list the emotional qualities you aspire to. For example, contentment, security, joy, an easy-relaxed, flexible way of being etc. Next list the emotional features of relationships you wish to attract to yourself and to show in your relationships with others. These may be people you know. For example, I wish to show my brother more patience, or they may be those you don't know as yet. For example, I wish to show my future employer my leadership skills.

The spiritual sense: consider the spiritual traditions and philosophies you wish to explore and live by, the spiritual attributes you would like to develop within yourself, and groups, courses, books etc. which may assist you to do/be so.

When completed give your focused attention to each item in turn on your vision board. As you do you might mantra affirmation words and place your hand over each. Visualize it in your life.

Reflect on your vision board. It is a creation in itself. Recall that which you have already created. Sense victorious, uplifted fulfillment.

My Journaling with Creator

Some of my favorite, beautiful and most powerful creation statements are:

I allow my highest good to effortlessly arrive as my highest good with the only expectation being my highest good.

I am an irresistible magnet with the power to attract to myself everything that I divinely desire according to the thoughts, feelings and pictures I constantly image and radiate; according to that which is for my highest learning, growth, potentials and prosperity; according to that of the highest good of others connected to me and this creation; and ultimately, according to the God-plan for my life.

I am a child of God, no less than the trees and the stars. I am beautiful, magnificent and essential and I am creating a magnificent life of deep joy and contribution in the perfect place, for the perfect pay, in perfect health, within the perfect relationships.

I dare to change, reform, and re-create my world congruent with my heart's desires and congruent with the God-heart which resides within me.

The work of my hands and the plans of my life are right now moving easily and quickly toward a sure and perfect fulfillment.

Nurture

Positive Experience: to feel nurtured, provided for, warmth, cared for, comforted, nursed, nourished, fed, clothed, sheltered, sustained, enfolded, held dear, fostered. Nurturing encompasses physical, mental, emotional, spiritual, familial, social and cultural needs.

Negative Experience: to feel ignored, rejected, disregarded, abandoned.

Journaling with Nurturer:

Your words for Nurture:

Check with which Mother of Origin you have experienced Nurture:

Biological Mother	
Significant Women or Men	
Community Organization Health Care	
Culture	
Mythological Spiritual Divine Church Mother Beings	
Mother Earth	
Your Inside Mother	
Other	

1. Choose one experience of being nurtured. Write its story, its time, place, feeling, conversation:

Complete with "I felt nurtured when I/he/she did/said.........."

2. Take an experience when you did not feel nurtured. Image and write:

3. Write how you would have liked this experience to be, in other words, rewrite that history:

4. What is it in the rewritten story that brings you a positive experience of nurture?

5. Take an item that brings you nurture and write a practical way to bring this to your mothering:

Identifying what nurtures you and ways to bring this to your mothering is your resource from your nurture mother of power.

Valerie Albrecht

Nurture Meditation:

Effect by nurturing your physical self in some way – have a bath, a swim, care for your body, dress lavishly.

Nurture your mental and emotional self by tending to your environment – play music, burn essences, decorate with flowers and talismen.

Nurture your spirit by

Lying Still.

Lying Easy.

Finding your breath.

Breathe In. Breathe Out.

Your breath always waits for you to remember her.

Breathe In. Breathe Out.

Imagine a waterfall cascading over grey black slates of rock dressed in lush leaves from dinosaur times.

Imagine the trickling of water on lichen rocks.

In the centre of the waterfall pool is a circle of sunlight.

See yourself swimming in the circle of sunlight, floating in the circle of sunlight. Your pores are open, your skin is tingling. You taste the pure water freshness. You smell its rejuvenation.

You are being embraced by the water nurturer.

See yourself filling a jug from the waterfall nurturer. What would be in this jug? A delicious table of food and drink? A massage? A holiday?

Then see yourself pouring the contents of this jug over yourself.

Re-fill your jug pouring its contents again and again over yourself until you are content.

Now see yourself swimming to the edge of the pool, climbing languidly out into another circle of sunlight.

Rest in this circle of sunlight with your eyes closed, smiling, perfectly, infinitely nurtured.

My Journaling with Nurturer

Nurturers of my physical, emotional and spiritual selves have been my teachers in yoga. It was these people who showed me how to create sacred space in which to listen to myself and discover my mothers of power. A lover nurtured my femininity through gifts when I had momentarily forgotten because of the demands of being a single mother of three. A work mentor nurtured my ideals for justice in health care. My teachers in writing nurtured my intellect and creativity. My mother nurtured my by once saying, "Look at this job you are in. You are not happy".

Protection

How we all desire safety from the "big bad wolves" of life!

In childhood we want our mothers to always have the band-aid and baked cakes, to always be at the same address, to be constant, consistent, present, available to look after us in our times of need, to act on our behalves in situations which seem insurmountable to us, to provide physical and emotional refuge and perfect, timely words of wisdom.

In adulthood we expect our employment, communities, churches and legal system to offer protection and security through occupational health and safety regulations; through enforcing laws and mores to live by, and of course by providing the monthly pay check.

As we age, we turn to both health workers and our children with the hope that they will offer us some protection and care.

In the bigger picture, we desire those we pray to, to provide security, safety and protection.

So it would seem that life appears to offer protection and yet we have all experienced abandonment at some time, over matters great, and matters small, and from many and varied sources.

It is not my purpose here to propose why this may be so. It is my purpose to offer to you this journaling process to clarify your Mother Power of Protection. Through writing and re-creating your protection experiences, both positive and negative, you may find what brings you protection and then be more able to provide protection for yourself and for those you desire to protect.

Positive Attributes: to fend for, to watch over, to care for, to keep safe, to preserve, to maintain, to desire to look after and provide refuge for those we care for, to shield, defend, save, secure, guard, preserve, safeguard.

Negative Attributes: to abandon and injure.

Journaling with Protection:

Your words for Protector:

Check with which Mother of Origin you have experienced Protection:

Biological Mother	
Significant Women or Men	
Community Organization Health Care	
Culture	
Mythological Spiritual Divine Church Mother Beings	
Mother Earth	
Your Inside Mother	
Other	

1. Choose one experience of being protected. Write its story, its time, place, feeling, conversation:

Complete with "I felt protected when I/he/she did/said........."

2. Take an experience when you did not feel protected. Image and write:

3. Write how you would have liked this experience to be, in other words, rewrite that history.

4. What is it in the rewritten story that brings you a positive experience of protection?

5. Take an item that brings you a feeling of protection. Write a practical way to bring this to your mothering:

Identifying what brings you protection and ways to bring this to your mothering is your resource from your protection mother of power.

Protection Meditation and Ceremony:

Affect by making your personal protection cards. Use the words from above which you chose for protection and also what and who you identified as providing you with protection. Write each on small cards referring to them when you feel the need for protection.

Valerie Albrecht

My Journaling with Protection

My mother protected me as a child by de-boning chicken and fish, by putting floaties on me when learning to swim, and by holding my hand when crossing roads. As a teenager she protected me by setting rules about staying out late. My ex-husband and subsequent lovers protected me by walking on the road side of the footpath, by advising about money and business, and through home maintenance to keep me safe. I have been protector for my children in all these ways. Now, I protect myself by staying in awareness of my boundaries and doing my best to live by them. This is an ongoing challenge, especially in a relationship, any relationship, because of my giving nature, my religious upbringing, and the model of my mother not knowing and/ or not protecting her own needs and boundaries.

Wisdom Teaching

The list of what biological mother teaches, by example or by omission of example, extends almost infinitely when we run the movie of our lives. Her teaching includes skills such as home making, cooking, sewing, knitting, cleaning and house keeping. It includes patterns of personal hygiene, dress sense, health care, studying, playing sport, and pursuing hobbies and interests. Her teaching on a more subtle level, is about the attributes of helping, caring, sharing, honesty, pride, success, patience, fun – extending, as I said, into an almost infinite list, all requiring wisdom to teach.

Then there are our other mother of origin wisdom teachers. School teachers are significant mother figures who teach us academia. Community mothers teach about giving and helping the less fortunate. Organization/employer mothers hopefully teach team work and fairness. Mother Nature will teach to respect her beauty and cycles. Spiritual, biblical, and mythological mothers teach compassion and forgiveness. And our inside mother teaches us when to rest, when to play, when to focus and when to trust. Of course these mothers may teach these things through both positive and negative experiences.

Ultimately mothers of origin are wisdom teachers of all the mother powers.

Positive Aspects: inspiration, awe, guidance, preparation, coaching, encouragement.

Negative Aspects: lack of the above.

2. Take an experience when you did not feel appropriately taught. Image and write:

3. Write how you would have liked this experience to be, in other words, rewrite that history:

4. What is it in the rewritten story that brings you a positive experience of teacher?

5. Take an experience which helped you feel positively taught and write a practical way of bringing this to your mothering:

Identifying who taught you and what and how you have been taught, are your resources from your mother of power wisdom teachers.

Wisdom Teaching Meditation and Ceremony:

Affect by listing as many things as you can, that you have been taught, and by which Mother of Origin. Complete by simply saying thank you.

My Journaling with Wisdom Teaching

Looking over my time with my mother, I am struck by the vastness and depth of what she, as wisdom teacher taught me and continues to teach me since her passing. And, that the experiences I perceive as negative, taught me as much or more than the positive ones. Her teaching was conscious through words, actions, behaviors, beliefs, ways of being, and unconscious through ways of not being. Her teaching was given from all her Mothers of Power and from all her Mothers of Origin to inspire, empower and enable me to mother, and to inspire, empower and enable my children in their turn, to mother. I am truly blessed.

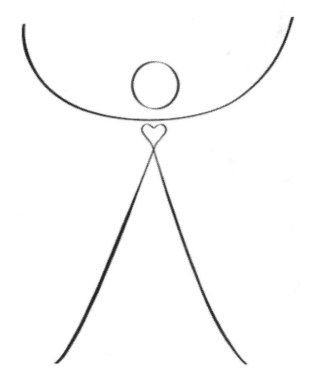

Understanding, writing and revising the place and wisdom of Mothers of Origin and Mothers of Powers in my life has shown me the beauty in all beings, has comforted me, inspired me and taught me to mother myself and mine — may it have done so for you. Thank you for Mother Journaling.

References

1. *Thirteen Mothers of Wisdom* by Jamie Sams
    Publ: Harper San Francisco 1993
2. *The Bible*
3. *Oxford Dictionary*
4. *Women of Grace and Power by Timothy Conway*
    Publ: Enlightened Spirituality.org 2006
5. *Women Who Run with the Wolves* by Clarissa Pinkola Estes
    Publ: Ballantine Books 1992